WOODLAND
WILDLIFE

Text/Consultant: Terence Lindsey
Illustrator: David Kirshner

Published by
The National Geographic Society
Reg Murphy, President and Chief Executive Officer
Gilbert M. Grosvenor, Chairman of the Board
Nina D. Hoffman, Senior Vice President
William R. Gray, Vice President and Director, Book Division
Barbara Lalicki, Director of Children's Publishing
Barbara Brownell, Senior Editor
Mark A. Caraluzzi, Marketing Manager
Vincent P. Ryan, Manufacturing Manager

Library of Congress Catalog Number: 96-068948
ISBN: 0-7922-3447-2

Produced for the National Geographic Society by Weldon Owen Pty Ltd
43 Victoria Street, McMahons Point, NSW 2060, Australia
A member of the Weldon Owen Group of Companies
Sydney • San Francisco

Chairman: Kevin Weldon
President: John Owen
Publisher: Sheena Coupe
Managing Editor: Ariana Klepac
Text Editor: Robert Coupe
Art Director: Sue Burk
Designer: Mark Thacker
Photo Researcher: Anne Ferrier
Production Manager: Caroline Webber

Film production by Mandarin Offset
Printed in Mexico

MY FIRST POCKET GUIDE

WOODLAND WILDLIFE

TERENCE LINDSEY

NATIONAL GEOGRAPHIC SOCIETY

INTRODUCTION

Trees are almost everywhere, but woodlands or forests are those places where trees grow close enough to touch, or almost touch, each other. Woodlands offer animals many places to shelter and feed. Some creatures live in the trees— on the bark or among the leaves. Some live on the ground in the undergrowth, and others live in or near streams or ponds.

There are two main types of American woodlands or forests, and they are easy to tell apart. In coniferous (co-NIF-uh-ruhs) forests the trees grow in conelike shapes, so the snow slides off and doesn't break the branches with its weight. The trees have thin, needlelike leaves all year round. In deciduous (di-SIJ-uh-wuhs) forests the leaves are broader, flatter, and softer. They drop off the trees in autumn, often changing color from green to red, yellow, or orange before they fall.

Woodland animals often hide, but you may see them if you are patient. Sometimes you don't need to see an animal to know it's there. You may be able to hear the sounds it makes, see its nest or den, or, in winter, find its tracks in the snow.

HOW TO USE THIS BOOK

This book is organized by type of animal. You will meet six different groups—spiders, insects, amphibians (am-FIB-ee-unz), reptiles, birds, and finally, mammals. Each spread in this book helps you to identify one kind of animal. It gives you information about the animal's size, color, appearance, and behavior. "Where To Find" has a map of North America that is shaded to show you where the animal lives. You can discover an unusual fact about the animal in the "Field Notes," and see it in its natural environment in the photograph. For all the mammals except the big brown bat, the animals' tracks, or paw prints, are shown to help you identify them. If you find a word you do not know, you can look it up in the Glossary on page 76.

ORB-WEAVING SPIDER

There are many different kinds of spiders, but the easiest to find are orb-weaving spiders. They spin large, round webs made from a sticky silk made inside their bodies.

WHERE TO FIND:
You can find these spiders almost anywhere in North America. Look for their webs strung between bushes.

WHAT TO LOOK FOR:

✳ **SIZE**
Orb-weaving spiders can be as small as a pinprick, or as big as a quarter.

✳ **COLOR**
Most are brown, black, or gray, but others are brightly colored.

✳ **BEHAVIOR**
A spider kills its prey using poison injected through its fangs when it bites.

✳ **MORE**
Insects get caught in the spider's sticky web. Then the spider eats the insects.

FIELD NOTES

When an insect gets caught in the web, the spider wraps the insect in silk to stop it from escaping.

Spiders are not insects. Just count the legs. Spiders have eight legs, while insects have six.

WOLF SPIDER

Not all spiders build webs to catch insects. A wolf spider stalks an insect and then pounces on it. Wolf spiders are just as common as orb-weaving spiders, but they are harder to find.

FIELD NOTES

A baby spider climbs to the top of a blade of grass, lets out some silk, and waits for a gust of wind to blow it away.

A wolf spider has eight eyes to help it see in many directions at once. It has two rows of two large eyes, and a row of four small eyes.

WHERE TO FIND:
You can find wolf spiders on the ground or on tree trunks almost anywhere in North America.

WHAT TO LOOK FOR:

✳ SIZE
With its legs spread out, a wolf spider measures up to about two inches across.

✳ COLOR
Most wolf spiders are grayish brown.

✳ BEHAVIOR
Some kinds of wolf spiders carry their babies around with them on their backs, to keep them safe.

✳ MORE
Wolf spiders are hard to see because they are the same color as their surroundings.

EASTERN TENT CATERPILLAR

 Large numbers of eastern tent caterpillars work together to weave a tentlike web over the twigs and branches of trees. This tent protects the caterpillars from their enemies.

WHERE TO FIND:
Eastern tent caterpillars are common across most of eastern North America. Look for their tents in trees.

WHAT TO LOOK FOR:

✳ SIZE
Eastern tent caterpillars are about two inches long.

✳ COLOR
They are mainly black, with yellow and green markings along their sides.

✳ BEHAVIOR
They mainly eat the leaves of crab apple, apple, and cherry trees. Their tents sometimes smother and kill trees.

✳ MORE
Their bodies are covered with tiny hairs.

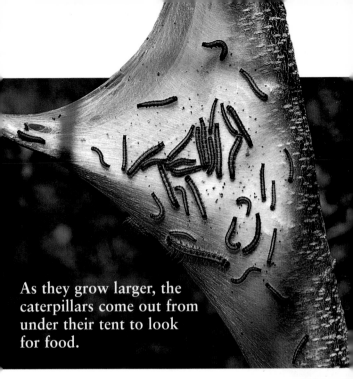

As they grow larger, the caterpillars come out from under their tent to look for food.

Moth

Caterpillar

MONARCH BUTTERFLY

 Like birds, monarch (MON-ark) butterflies fly south to warmer climates to spend the winter. Huge swarms of monarch butterflies make the trip south together, returning in spring.

WHERE TO FIND:
Monarch butterflies are found from North through Central America. Look for the striped caterpillars.

WHAT TO LOOK FOR:

✳ **SIZE**
A monarch butterfly is four inches from wingtip to wingtip.

✳ **COLOR**
Its wings are bright orange, with black lines and white spots.

✳ **BEHAVIOR**
Its flight is slow, fluttery, and graceful. Sometimes it soars through the air.

✳ **MORE**
The caterpillars eat poisonous leaves so they taste bad and birds won't eat them.

Monarch butterflies often visit flowers to sip their nectar.

○○○○○○○○○○○○○

FIELD NOTES

In winter these
butterflies cluster
on tree trunks,
from the southern
United States
to Central America.

SPRING PEEPER

A chorus of piping whistles at dusk near a pond or swamp, is a sure sign that spring has arrived. This is the call of the spring peeper—a frog that is easy to hear, but hard to find. Frogs are amphibians (am-FIB-ee-uhnz). Amphibians live on land but lay their eggs in water.

FIELD NOTES

Tiny, sticky pads at the ends of its long toes help a spring peeper to cling to plants and other objects.

WHERE TO FIND:

The spring peeper lives in much of eastern and midwestern North America. Look near ponds or swamps during spring.

WHAT TO LOOK FOR:

✳ SIZE
A spring peeper is about one inch long.

✳ COLOR
It is greenish gray or brown, with a faint, dark-colored X on its back.

✳ BEHAVIOR
To attract a mate, the male inflates a balloonlike sac on his throat. This makes his call louder and helps it carry farther.

✳ MORE
The spring peeper feeds on small insects.

The male inflates the sac on his throat, like a balloon.

WOOD FROG

The soft call of the wood frog sounds a little like a duck's quack. This frog sometimes lives a long way from water, but returns to ponds and streams to breed. It eats insects, spiders, and crustaceans.

WHERE TO FIND:
Wood frogs are found throughout most of northern North America in grasslands and moist woodlands.

WHAT TO LOOK FOR:

＊ SIZE
Wood frogs grow about three inches long—as long as a baseball card.

＊ COLOR
They vary in color from pale brown to almost black with a white belly and reddish brown bands on the legs.

＊ BEHAVIOR
The wood frog hibernates during winter.

＊ MORE
Frogs have strong back legs that make them good jumpers.

The wood frog has a dark patch, like a bandit's mask, on its face.

FIELD NOTES

Like all frogs, wood frogs begin life as tadpoles. Tadpoles look a bit like fish and swim in water.

EASTERN HOGNOSE SNAKE

 Like all snakes, the eastern hognose snake is a reptile. Its snout is upturned like a hog's. It uses it like a shovel to dig toads and frogs out of their burrows.

WHERE TO FIND:
The eastern hognose snake lives in the eastern half of the United States. Look in areas with sandy soil.

WHAT TO LOOK FOR:

✳ SIZE
Hognose snakes grow to three feet long.

✳ COLOR
Most are a dull yellowish brown, with big blackish spots.

✳ BEHAVIOR
When threatened, a hognose snake may swallow air to puff itself up and hiss loudly to frighten off an attacker.

✳ MORE
Snakes gather smells from the air through scent organs in their tongues.

A hognose snake is the same color as the leaves on the woodland floor. This makes it hard for predators to see.

FIELD NOTES

If attacked, a hognose snake may roll over and pretend to be dead, hoping the predator will go away.

EASTERN BOX TURTLE

 When the weather is hot and dry the eastern box turtle burrows under fallen logs to keep cool. Like all turtles, it is a reptile. Eastern box turtles can live for up to a hundred years.

Bright markings show that this turtle is young. The markings fade with age.

FIELD NOTES

A box turtle can pull its body back into its shell and tightly shut the shell to protect itself from enemies.

WHERE TO FIND:
The eastern box turtle lives in the eastern and midwestern United States, in woodlands, pastures, and floodplains.

WHAT TO LOOK FOR:

✶ SIZE
The eastern box turtle can grow about six inches long.

✶ COLOR
Its shell is mainly black or very dark brown, with light brown, dull red, or yellowish markings.

✶ BEHAVIOR
Eastern box turtles often lie soaking in shallow water or mud.

✶ MORE
They eat plants and animals.

WOOD DUCK

 The wood duck lives near ponds and streams in the woods. In fall, it leaves its summer home to spend the winter in Mexico and the southern states, where it is warmer. In spring, it returns.

WHERE TO FIND:
In warm months, wood ducks live in parts of the United States and Canada. They fly South for winter.

WHAT TO LOOK FOR:

✳ **SIZE**
A wood duck is about 18 inches long.

✳ **COLOR**
The male has a pattern of bright colors, but the female is mostly dull brown.

✳ **BEHAVIOR**
Wood ducks nest in holes high up in dead trees. Their call can be a loud *wooo-eeek* or a soft *peet* or *cheep*.

✳ **MORE**
You can often see wood ducks perching on the branches of trees.

After breeding, this male will lose his bright feathers and become a dull brown color.

FIELD NOTES

When her eggs hatch, the female calls to the ducklings high in the tree to jump from the nest.

RUFFED GROUSE

The ruff—or collar—of brownish black feathers on its neck gives the ruffed grouse its name. When it sees you, the ruffed grouse will usually burst into flight with a loud roar of its wings.

FIELD NOTES

Males stand on fallen logs and beat their wings to attract females. The sound is like distant thunder.

WHERE TO FIND:
Ruffed grouse live in dense forests, abandoned farms, and overgrown fields across northern North America.

WHAT TO LOOK FOR:

✳ SIZE
A ruffed grouse is about 17 inches long.

✳ COLOR
It is a dull gray or reddish brown color. Its tail has a dark gray band near the tip.

✳ BEHAVIOR
It eats buds, shoots, and other similar parts of plants.

✳ MORE
A ruffed grouse sometimes plunges headfirst into a snow bank to escape a pursuing predator.

Most ruffed grouse have gray tails, like this one. But some have reddish tails.

WILD TURKEY

 Because humans hunt wild turkeys, these birds hide from people. Wild turkeys search on the ground for acorns, insects, and similar food. Wild turkeys often roost on branches overhanging water.

WHERE TO FIND:
Wild turkeys live in open woodlands in many parts of the United States and Mexico. They live in small flocks.

WHAT TO LOOK FOR:

✱ SIZE
Male turkeys are nearly four feet long.

✱ COLOR
Their feathers are deep brown, with a rich green and red gloss.

✱ BEHAVIOR
The wild turkey makes a loud gobbling sound. It also makes clucks and yelps.

✱ MORE
A wild turkey's head is pink and has no feathers. Dangling bits of red skin under the bird's beak are called wattles.

A male struts with its feathers fluffed and its tail spread wide, trying to attract a female.

Female

BARRED OWL

At night the barred owl hunts for mice and other small animals. It has huge eyes that help it to see in the dark. By day it sleeps in a leafy tree. But if you startle it, you may see it fly off to find another perch.

The barred owl gets its name from the bars, or striped feathers, on its upper chest.

WHAT TO LOOK FOR:

✷ SIZE
A barred owl is about 21 inches long.

✷ COLOR
It is dull gray-brown, with white spots above and blackish streaks underneath.

✷ BEHAVIOR
Its call is a series of low hoots, which sound a bit like *Who cooks for you? Who cooks for you all?* You may hear this call late in the afternoon.

✷ MORE
The female nests in hollow trees.

FIELD NOTES

If small birds come across a roosting barred owl during the day, they may mob and pester it.

29

YELLOW-BELLIED SAPSUCKER

The yellow-bellied sapsucker is a kind of woodpecker. It drills holes in the bark of trees. Sap oozes from the holes, which the bird then drinks. This habit gives the bird its name.

WHERE TO FIND:
The yellow-bellied sapsucker lives around North America, but in winter it flies south to Central America.

WHAT TO LOOK FOR:

✳ SIZE
The yellow-bellied sapsucker is just under nine inches long.

✳ COLOR
It has a pattern of black, white, red, and yellow feathers. It has a yellow belly and white wing stripes.

✳ BEHAVIOR
As it hops up the trunks of trees, it leans back on its stiff tail for balance.

✳ MORE
It searches tree trunks for insects to eat.

The sapsucker has a long, strong, pointed beak to help it dig holes in trees.

FIELD NOTES

The sapsucker drills its sap holes in neat rows in the bark. It's easy to see where the bird has been.

OVENBIRD

Small and brown, the ovenbird is hard to see against the undergrowth on the forest floor, where it lives. But it is easy to hear. Its loud, ringing song sounds like *teacher-teacher-TEACHER*.

Ovenbirds spend most of their time on the ground in shaded, sheltered places.

WHERE TO FIND:
The ovenbird is common in dense forests across North America. It spends the winter in Central and South America.

WHAT TO LOOK FOR:

✳ SIZE
An ovenbird is about as long as this book is tall.

✳ COLOR
It is brown above and white below. It has bold, black streaks on its breast.

✳ BEHAVIOR
It feeds on insects and small spiders. Its song is often heard at night.

✳ MORE
It has a rust-colored crown and a white ring around its eye.

FIELD NOTES
The ovenbird is named after its rounded, roofed nest, which looks a little like a tiny, pioneer's oven.

SCARLET TANAGER

 The scarlet tanager (TAN-uh-jer) is a long-distance traveler. It leaves North America in fall to fly to Central and South America for the winter. The male is one of the most colorful North American birds.

WHERE TO FIND:
The scarlet tanager lives in treetops in woodlands in the eastern half of North America. It flies south for winter.

WHAT TO LOOK FOR:

✳ SIZE
A scarlet tanager is about seven inches long—about as long as a pencil.

✳ COLOR
The male has a bright red body, but its wings and tail are black.

✳ BEHAVIOR
The scarlet tanager feeds mainly on insects, but also eats berries. It sometimes visits garden bird feeders.

✳ MORE
It has a pale yellowish bill.

The male scarlet tanager helps the female collect food for their three or four babies.

Female

FIELD NOTES

Females look much like males but for color and wing pattern. The male is red and the female is yellowish green.

GRAY JAY

 Wherever there are lots of pine and spruce trees, gray jays are common, even in winter. Gray jays are showy birds and often perch at the tops of trees. They are bold and tame around humans.

WHERE TO FIND:
The gray jay lives in evergreen forests across Canada, and in parts of the western United States.

WHAT TO LOOK FOR:

✳ **SIZE**
A gray jay is just under one foot long.

✳ **COLOR**
It is mainly gray with a whitish underside, a white crown, and a black nape.

✳ **BEHAVIOR**
It is sometimes called the whiskey jack, because of its call *whiskey jack*.

✳ **MORE**
It eats mainly seeds and will store seeds away in summer to eat in winter, when food is hard to find.

The gray jay has fluffy, gray feathers and a long tail.

FIELD NOTES

The gray jay often steals food from picnic tables. It may even enter campers' tents to find food.

VIRGINIA OPOSSUM

If threatened, the Virginia opossum may fall down and pretend to be dead so the attacker will go away. To "play possum" means to pretend to be dead or asleep. Virginia opossums are active at night.

FIELD NOTES

When young opossums grow too big for their mother's pouch, they crawl out and cling to her fur.

An opossum's body has coarse, shaggy fur, its face has smooth fur, and its paws and tail have no fur.

WHERE TO FIND:
The Virginia opossum lives as far south as Central America. It is rare in deserts, mountains, and prairies.

WHAT TO LOOK FOR:

✳ SIZE
Not counting the tail, Virginia opossums grow about 20 inches long.

✳ COLOR
They are pale gray with white faces.

✳ BEHAVIOR
The opossum is a kind of mammal called a marsupial (mar-SOO-pee-uhl). Marsupial mothers carry their babies in furry pouches on their bodies.

✳ MORE
They eat mainly plants and vegetables.

39

BIG BROWN BAT

Although bats have wings, they are mammals. Many different kinds of bats live in North America, but the big brown bat is the biggest. Bats feed at night on flying insects such as moths and beetles.

WHERE TO FIND:
You can find big brown bats in woods and forests throughout most of North America.

WHAT TO LOOK FOR:

✳ **SIZE**
A big brown bat measures about eight inches across, from wingtip to wingtip.

✳ **COLOR**
It has glossy, dark brown fur.

✳ **BEHAVIOR**
The big brown bat is the fastest bat. It can fly up to 40 miles per hour.

✳ **MORE**
Bats' wings don't have feathers. Their wings are made of leathery skin stretched between long, thin fingers.

When they are roosting, bats hang upside down, dangling by their feet. Bats roost in hollow trees, caves, and buildings.

FIELD NOTES

Some mammals can glide through the air, but bats are the only mammals that can truly fly.

RED FOX

Red foxes are most active at dawn and at dusk, but you may sometimes catch a glimpse of them during the day. At night you might hear a red fox's high-pitched bark.

FIELD NOTES

When a fox hears prey underground, it jumps up, then lands with all four paws together, trapping the prey in its hole.

Notice the red fox's alert ears, slim muzzle, bushy tail, and black, "stockinged" feet.

WHERE TO FIND:
You can find red foxes throughout most of North America. They can even survive in big cities.

WHAT TO LOOK FOR:

✳ SIZE
A red fox grows a little over three feet long—the size of a small dog.

✳ COLOR
It is reddish brown, with black paws. It has a long, bushy, white-tipped tail.

✳ BEHAVIOR
Young red fox pups stay with their mother in the den, while the father fetches food for the whole family.

✳ MORE
Red foxes hunt small animals and birds.

BLACK BEAR

Big, shaggy black bears have a good sense of smell, but they cannot see well. They tear open beehives with their strong paws, then eat the honey and bees inside. They eat a range of other foods from berries to birds.

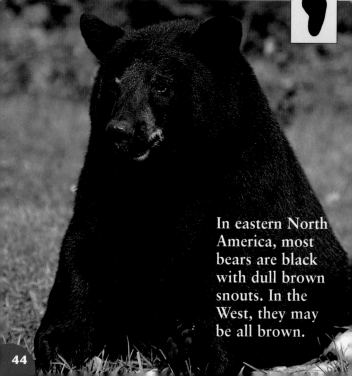

In eastern North America, most bears are black with dull brown snouts. In the West, they may be all brown.

The black bear lives in forests, swamps, and wooded mountains across Canada and in parts of the United States.

WHAT TO LOOK FOR:

✳ SIZE
A black bear is about three feet tall when on all fours. It is much taller when it rears up on its hind legs.

✳ COLOR
Most black bears are black, but some are brown, or even dull white.

✳ BEHAVIOR
They sometimes hang around garbage dumps or picnic areas, looking for food.

✳ MORE
Some have a white patch on the chest.

FIELD NOTES

Despite their large size, black bears climb trees easily by gripping the bark with their sharp claws.

45

RACCOON

Often called a ringtail because of its ringed tail, the raccoon (ra-KOON), or coon, is common in woodlands. Its calls include growls, snarls, and a soft, twittering sound that females use to comfort their babies.

FIELD NOTES

Raccoons often take their food to a nearby stream or pond to wash it carefully before eating it.

A raccoon usually lives close to a pond, river, or stream.

WHERE TO FIND:
Raccoons range from southern Canada to Central America. They are mainly active at night.

WHAT TO LOOK FOR:

✳ SIZE
A raccoon grows a little over three feet long, from its nose to the tip of its tail.

✳ COLOR
It is gray, with a black mask and dark bands around its tail.

✳ BEHAVIOR
In winter, raccoons often hide away in burrows or dens to keep warm.

✳ MORE
Raccoons eat almost anything. They often raid garbage cans in cities.

STRIPED SKUNK

You will probably smell a striped skunk before you see it! It squirts a nasty-smelling spray from under its tail into the face of an attacker. The striped skunk lives on the ground and eats mice and other small animals. It is active at night.

FIELD NOTES

When threatened, a skunk turns its back, raises and fans out its tail, and sprays its attacker.

WHAT TO LOOK FOR:

✳ SIZE
A skunk is about as big as a house cat.

✳ COLOR
It is black, with a white patch on its head and a white stripe along each side.

✳ BEHAVIOR
A female usually has five or six cubs, which follow her around in single file.

✳ MORE
A skunk stamps its feet to warn an attacker that it is about to spray. If the warning is ignored, the skunk sprays.

The skunk's bold markings warn enemies to keep away, or they might get sprayed.

BOBCAT

A bobcat looks like a large, muscular house cat. It is rarely seen, but you may find its tracks in the snow. It hunts birds and mammals. Cottontail rabbits are its favorite prey.

FIELD NOTES

A bobcat hunts by lying in wait for its victim, or by quietly stalking and then pouncing on its prey.

Notice the bobcat's pointed ears.

WHERE TO FIND:
The bobcat lives in woodlands in most of Mexico and the United States, and in southern Canada.

WHAT TO LOOK FOR:

✳ SIZE
A bobcat grows about three feet long, including its short tail.

✳ COLOR
It has brown fur covered with small blackish spots.

✳ BEHAVIOR
It lives in a den under a fallen log, or in some other hidden place.

✳ MORE
It gets its name from its tail, which looks "bobbed," or cut short.

WHITE-TAILED DEER

The white-tailed deer gets its name from the white underside of its tail. When running away from danger, the deer lifts its tail to show this white fur. This warns other deer.

FIELD NOTES

These deer can run 40 miles an hour, leap 30 feet forward in one bound, and jump nearly 9 feet into the air.

Only male white-tailed deer have antlers. They grow a new set every year.

WHERE TO FIND:
The white-tailed deer is found in woods and forests almost everywhere in North America.

WHAT TO LOOK FOR:

✳ SIZE
An adult male white-tailed deer stands about three feet high at the shoulders.

✳ COLOR
Males are gray and females are reddish. Fawns are reddish with pale spots.

✳ BEHAVIOR
White-tailed deer feed mainly on grass, twigs, and acorns.

✳ MORE
Wolves and cougars (KOO-gerz) hunt white-tailed deer for food.

MULE DEER

 The mule (MYOOL) deer feeds on plants and grasses. When threatened, it runs away holding its tail low, which forms a black "bull's-eye" in a circle of white fur. Mule deer are hunted by wolves.

WHERE TO FIND:
Mule deer live almost everywhere in western North America, wherever there are trees or shrubs.

WHAT TO LOOK FOR:

✳ SIZE
Mule deer are about the same size as white-tailed deer.

✳ COLOR
A mule deer has gray fur, a black muzzle, and small black hooves.

✳ BEHAVIOR
Mule deer feed mainly at dawn and dusk, but you might see them at any time of day.

✳ MORE
The males grow new antlers each year.

The mule deer has white fur on its rump and its tail has a black tip.

FIELD NOTES

Male mule deer have antlers. In fall, they use the antlers to fight other males for females to mate with.

MOOSE

A moose is a sort of deer, but it is much bigger than any other kind. It feeds on leaves, bark, and plant shoots. The male has large, flat antlers that grow in fall and drop out in winter.

FIELD NOTES
Moose like water and are strong swimmers. They can swim faster than a canoeist can paddle.

Moose usually live close to a lake, pond, or river, especially in summer, so they can keep cool.

WHERE TO FIND:
Moose live across Canada and in some northern parts of the United States. They are most active at night.

WHAT TO LOOK FOR:

✳ SIZE
A moose is about as big as a horse.

✳ COLOR
It is dark grayish brown with long, pale legs and a stubby tail.

✳ BEHAVIOR
Moose often wade into ponds and rivers to eat water plants.

✳ MORE
A moose has a blunt, bulblike muzzle and a flap of skin and hair dangling from its throat, called a dewlap.

GRAY SQUIRREL

The gray squirrel (SKWER-uhl) feeds during the day, mainly on nuts and berries. At night it sleeps inside a hollow tree, in a woodpecker hole, or in branches, in a nest it builds out of leaves.

WHERE TO FIND:
The gray squirrel lives across much of the eastern United States and in southeastern Canada.

WHAT TO LOOK FOR:

✳ **SIZE**
The gray squirrel grows about 20 inches long, including its tail.

✳ **COLOR**
Its fur is grayish all over, but is a little paler underneath.

✳ **BEHAVIOR**
It often comes down from the trees to feed on the ground, but it runs back up if it is alarmed.

✳ **MORE**
It is often found in parks and gardens.

The gray squirrel's long, bushy tail helps the animal keep its balance.

FIELD NOTES

The gray squirrel buries acorns in the ground to eat later. It may forget where they are buried.

59

SOUTHERN FLYING SQUIRREL

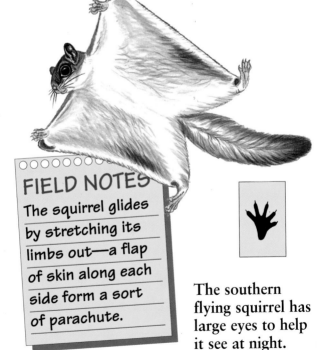

The southern flying squirrel glides through the air from one tree to another. It sleeps during the day, then comes out of its den around dusk to search for nuts and seeds.

The southern flying squirrel has large eyes to help it see at night.

WHERE TO FIND:
The southern flying squirrel is common in woodlands across the eastern half of the United States.

WHAT TO LOOK FOR:

☀ SIZE
The southern flying squirrel grows about ten inches long, including its tail.

☀ COLOR
Its fur is grayish brown, with a white underside.

☀ BEHAVIOR
It usually builds its den in a woodpecker hole in a tree. In cold weather, it may live in the attic of a building.

☀ MORE
It has soft fur and a long, furry tail.

EASTERN CHIPMUNK

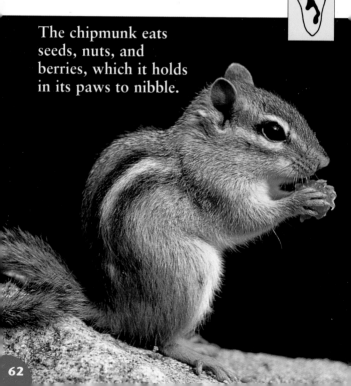

Most squirrels live in trees, but the eastern chipmunk is a kind of squirrel that lives in a burrow in the ground. It hibernates in its burrow during winter and also stores food there.

The chipmunk eats seeds, nuts, and berries, which it holds in its paws to nibble.

WHERE TO FIND:
The eastern chipmunk lives across most of southeastern Canada and the eastern United States.

WHAT TO LOOK FOR:

✳ SIZE
The eastern chipmunk's head and body are about six inches long. Its tail measures about three inches.

✳ COLOR
It is reddish brown with bold buff and blackish stripes along its sides.

✳ BEHAVIOR
Its call is a chatter that sounds rather like *chuck-chuck-chuck*.

✳ MORE
It has cheek pouches to store food in.

FIELD NOTES

When it is running, a chipmunk often holds its long, bushy tail straight up in the air.

WOODCHUCK

In many parts of North America, woodchucks are known as groundhogs. During the day they eat green grass and young plant shoots. At night, they sleep. Their call is a shrill whistle.

FIELD NOTES
Woodchucks go into their burrows in October and hibernate there until February.

Woodchucks often sit still and upright near their burrows, watching for danger.

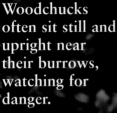

WHERE TO FIND:
Woodchucks live in most of Canada and in some eastern and midwestern states, in woodlands and fields.

WHAT TO LOOK FOR:

✳ SIZE
A woodchuck grows about two feet long from head to tail.

✳ COLOR
It has dull yellowish brown or grayish brown fur, and blackish feet.

✳ BEHAVIOR
It lives in a long, underground burrow with up to 11 entrances.

✳ MORE
Folklore says that if it sees its shadow on February 2, spring will soon come.

BEAVER

A stick-and-mud dam across a stream is a sure sign that beavers are nearby. The dam causes the water upstream to form a pond, where the beavers build their shelter, called a lodge. The entrance is underwater.

FIELD NOTES

Beavers work in pairs to build dams. They can swim underwater with sticks in their mouths.

A beaver's thick, waterproof fur keeps it dry in the water.

Beavers live in woodland ponds and streams across most of Canada and the United States.

WHAT TO LOOK FOR:

✴ SIZE
An old male beaver may be 40 inches long, from its nose to the tip of its tail.

✴ COLOR
A beaver's fur is dark brown all over.

✴ BEHAVIOR
Beavers eat bark. They chew saplings into chunks and carry them to their lodge to store them.

✴ MORE
A beaver has a flat, scaly, furless tail. It is paddle-shaped to help the beaver swim.

WHITE-FOOTED MOUSE

 There are many kinds of mice in North America, and most are hard to tell apart. The white-footed mouse is one of the most common. It gets its name from its white feet.

WHERE TO FIND:
The white-footed mouse lives in most of the central and eastern parts of North America.

WHAT TO LOOK FOR:

✱ SIZE
The white-footed mouse grows about as long as this book is tall. Its tail is about the same length as its body.

✱ COLOR
It is reddish brown on top, but its belly and feet are white.

✱ BEHAVIOR
It drums its forefeet quickly if scared.

✱ MORE
It stores food in fall to eat during the winter when food is scarce.

Berries are one of the mouse's favorite foods. It also eats seeds, nuts, and insects.

69

MUSKRAT

Lakes and rivers are home to the muskrat, which spends most of its time in water. It feeds mainly on water plants, but also eats frogs, small fish, and other small water animals.

The muskrat looks like a beaver, but it is smaller and has a thin tail.

WHAT TO LOOK FOR:

✹ SIZE
A muskrat's body is about two feet long, including its tail.

✹ COLOR
It has thick, soft, dark brown fur.

✹ BEHAVIOR
The entrance to a muskrat's lodge is underwater, to keep predators out. It also lives in burrows in riverbanks.

✹ MORE
Its hind feet are slightly webbed, like a duck's, to help it swim.

71

PORCUPINE

 The spiny porcupine (POR-kyuh-pine) eats the bark of trees. It is active mainly at night, but during the day you may see it hunched in a sort of blackish ball on a branch near the top of a tree.

WHERE TO FIND:
The porcupine lives in forests across the midwestern and northeastern United States, and also in Mexico.

WHAT TO LOOK FOR:

✳ SIZE
Porcupines grow about 30 inches long.

✳ COLOR
They have black or dark brown fur and yellowish, black, or brown spines, called quills (KWILZ).

✳ BEHAVIOR
The porcupine relies on its sharp quills for protection because it cannot run away quickly from predators.

✳ MORE
It has about 30,000 quills on its body.

A porcupine's long, pale, sharp quills almost hide its dark fur.

EASTERN COTTONTAIL

The eastern cottontail is a kind of rabbit. It gets its name from its short, fluffy white tail which looks like cotton. It has eyes on the side of its head that help it to watch for danger in many directions at once.

FIELD NOTES

Cottontail rabbits are born in shallow nests of leaves in the ground. Babies have no fur and are blind.

When it senses danger, a cottontail stays very still, listening for any sound.

WHERE TO FIND:
The eastern cottontail lives in much of North America and Central America. It is active at night and in the early morning.

WHAT TO LOOK FOR:

✳ SIZE
An eastern cottontail rabbit grows about 16 inches long. It has long ears.

✳ COLOR
It has dull, grayish brown fur, with paler feet. It has a rust-colored nape.

✳ BEHAVIOR
The cottontail usually hops, but it can also leap 10 to 15 feet at a time.

✳ MORE
It feeds mainly on grass, and also bark and twigs.

GLOSSARY

Amphibian A cold-blooded animal, such as a frog or toad, that lives on land but lays eggs in water.

Breed To mate and produce young.

Call Any sound made by an animal.

Cheek pouch A pocket of skin inside the mouth of some animals, used to store food.

Chorus The sound made when a group of animals calls together.

Cougar The largest kind of cat in North America, also known as the mountain lion or puma.

Crustacean A hard-shelled creature that usually lives in water and has many legs, such as a crab or crayfish.

Hibernate To sleep through the winter.

Inflate To swell up with air.

Mammal A warm-blooded animal, usually with hair or fur, that feeds its young on milk from the mother's body.

Nape The back of the neck.

Nectar The sweet fluid produced by flowers.

Predator Any animal that hunts other animals for food.

Prey Any animal hunted by other animals for food.

Reptile A cold-blooded animal with scaly or leathery skin, that usually lays eggs. The snake is an example.

Roost The place where an animal sleeps.

Ruff Thick fur or feathers around an animal's neck.

Sac A pouch or pocket of skin.

Sap The fluid inside a plant.

Sapling A young tree.

Song A special kind of call made by birds to attract a mate.

Stalk To follow quietly when hunting.

Undergrowth The lowest level of plants in a woodland or forest.

INDEX OF
WOODLAND
WILDLIFE

ABOUT THE CONSULTANT

Terence Lindsey was born in England but raised and educated in Canada. He has traveled widely in North America, Europe, and Australasia, but has made Australia his home for the past 25 years. He now lives in Sydney. His interests encompass most of the natural world, but he has studied, written, and taught mainly about birds, with a special interest in avian zoogeography and foraging and reproduction strategies. He is an Associate of the Australian Museum and a former tutor at the University of Sydney, but now devotes most of his time to writing, traveling, and consulting.

PHOTOGRAPHIC CREDITS